# What's the Issue?

# WHAT'S DRUG ABUSE?

By Richard Alexander

KidHaven
PUBLISHING

Published in 2019 by
**KidHaven Publishing, an Imprint of Greenhaven Publishing, LLC**
353 3rd Avenue
Suite 255
New York, NY 10010

Copyright © 2019 KidHaven Publishing, an Imprint of Greenhaven Publishing, LLC.

Designer: Andrea Davison-Bartolotta
Editor: Katie Kawa

Photo credits: Cover (top) Robert Kneschke/Shutterstock.com; cover (bottom) Ben Carlson/ Shutterstock.com; pp. 5 (main), 7 Photographee.eu/Shutterstock.com; p. 5 (inset) Bokeh Blur Background/Shutterstock.com; p. 9 (left inset) chombosan/Shutterstock.com; p. 9 (right inset) robin2/ Shutterstock.com; p. 9 (main) George Rudy/Shutterstock.com; p. 10 Don Carl STEFFEN/Gamma-Rapho via Getty Images; p. 11 (inset) MANDEL NGAN/AFP/Getty Images; p. 11 (right) legacy1995/ Shutterstock.com; p. 11 (left) TFoxFoto/Shutterstock.com; p. 12 young84/iStock/Thinkstock; p. 13 Joseph Sohm/Shutterstock.com; p. 15 Rocketclips, Inc./Shutterstock.com; p. 17 rikkyall/ Shutterstock.com; p. 18 Jupiterimages/Creatas/Thinkstock; p. 19 Elena Nichizhenova/ Shutterstock.com; p. 20 Robert Mora/Getty Images; p. 21 Creativika Graphics/Shutterstock.com.

**Library of Congress Cataloging-in-Publication Data**

Names: Alexander, Richard, author.
Title: What's drug abuse? / Richard Alexander.
Description: New York : KidHaven Publishing, [2019] | Series: What's the
  issue? | Includes index.
Identifiers: LCCN 2018017831 (print) | LCCN 2018018421 (ebook) | ISBN
  9781534527997 (eBook) | ISBN 9781534527980 (library bound book) | ISBN
  9781534527966 (pbk. book) | ISBN 9781534527973 (6 pack)
Subjects: LCSH: Drug abuse–United States–Juvenile literature. | Drug
  addiction–United States–Juvenile literature.
Classification: LCC HV5809.5 (ebook) | LCC HV5809.5 A43 2019 (print) | DDC
  362.290973–dc23
LC record available at https://lccn.loc.gov/2018017831

Printed in the United States of America

CPSIA compliance information: Batch #BW19KL: For further information contact Greenhaven Publishing LLC, New York, New York at 1-844-317-7404.

Please visit our website, www.greenhavenpublishing.com. For a free color catalog of all our high-quality books, call toll free 1-844-317-7404 or fax 1-844-317-7405.

# CONTENTS

# Helpful or Harmful?

It's important to take care of your body. In some cases, that means using drugs when you're sick to help you get healthy again. However, drugs that are helpful when you're sick can also be harmful when they're not used properly. Also, not all drugs are good for your body. In fact, many drugs can hurt you, and some are even illegal.

Drug abuse happens when people use illegal drugs or use legal drugs in a dangerous, or unsafe, way. Drug abuse is a big problem around the world, but people are working hard to find ways to stop it.

## Facing the Facts

People who abuse drugs have a substance use disorder. Doctors use those words to describe a person whose drug use is causing problems with their health and their ability to do what they need to do at work, home, or school.

The best way to fight against drug abuse is to stay away from harmful drugs and to only use helpful drugs in healthy ways.

# Understanding Addiction

When people talk about drug abuse, they often talk about addiction, too. People who abuse drugs can become addicted to them, which means they feel they need to keep using a drug even though it's harming them. People who are addicted to drugs can't control their drug use. Addiction often **affects** not only the person directly dealing with it, but also their family and friends.

People who are addicted to drugs have a disease, or a kind of sickness, that affects their brain. They need a doctor or another **professional** who deals with addiction to help them recover, or get better.

### Facing the Facts

An overdose happens when a person takes too much of a drug. In some cases, an overdose can send a person to the hospital or even kill them.

Addiction is a kind of sickness. If someone is addicted to drugs, that doesn't mean they're a bad person. It means they need help.

# The Dangers of Drinking and Smoking

People can abuse and become addicted to many kinds of drugs. Alcohol is often considered a drug because it affects how the brain and body work. People abuse alcohol when they drink too much of it, and they can become addicted to it. When adults drink alcohol **responsibly**, it doesn't harm them or anyone else. However, alcohol abuse can harm a person's body, and it can hurt their family and friends, too.

Another drug people often become addicted to is nicotine, which is found in **cigarettes** and other products. Smoking cigarettes can make people very sick.

## Facing the Facts

Some people believe vaping, or using **electronic** cigarettes, is safer than smoking other kinds of cigarettes. However, electronic cigarettes—also known as e-cigarettes—still put nicotine and other harmful **chemicals** into a person's body.

Many products that have alcohol and nicotine in them are legal for people over a certain age to buy. These products are illegal for kids and teenagers because they're harmful, and they can also be harmful for adults. For example, it can be deadly for a person to drive after they've had too much alcohol.

**NO VAPING**

**DON'T DRINK AND DRIVE**

# Illegal Drugs

Alcohol and nicotine are examples of drugs that are legal for adults over a certain age. However, many other drugs are illegal because they're so dangerous. Drug abuse includes using any of these illegal drugs over a period of time. Many illegal drugs are also very addictive, and they can cause a lot of damage, or harm, to a person's body.

Governments around the world want to **protect** their citizens from harmful drugs. In the United States, the Drug Enforcement Administration (DEA) is the part of the government that works to stop the creation and sale of illegal drugs.

## Facing the Facts

In the 1970s, President Richard Nixon said the United States was going to begin what's been called the war on drugs. Since then, the United States has spent more than $1 trillion fighting this war on drug use, abuse, and crime.

10

When people make, buy, or sell illegal drugs, they can go to jail.

11

# Making It Legal

Americans have different points of view about making certain drugs legal or illegal. **Marijuana** is an example of one of these drugs. Different states have different laws about marijuana use.

Some leaders believe all marijuana use is dangerous drug abuse, so they've made it illegal in their states. In other states, marijuana use is illegal unless it's used as medicine, or a drug that helps people when they're sick. Finally, some states have made responsible marijuana use legal in a way that's similar to how states treat alcohol.

## Facing the Facts

In 1996, California became the first U.S. state to legalize marijuana, or make it legal, when it's used as medicine.

In the United States, citizens vote on laws about legalizing certain drugs.

13

# Drugs from the Doctor

The use of illegal drugs is a big part of the drug abuse problem in the United States. Another part of the problem is the misuse of drugs that doctors give people when they're sick or in pain. These are called prescription drugs.

Prescription drug abuse can often lead to addiction. This is especially true for drugs that are meant to take away pain. Many of those prescription drugs are part of a group of drugs called opioids. When people become addicted to prescription opioids, they sometimes begin using illegal opioids, such as a drug called heroin. This drug is very dangerous.

## Facing the Facts

A 2017 study showed that opioid overdoses kill more than 115 Americans every day.

A doctor's directions should always be followed when taking prescription drugs. Taking too much of a drug, taking it more often than directed, and taking it when it's not needed are all ways that prescription drugs are abused.

15

# A National Problem

A person who abuses opioids has an opioid use disorder. As of 2016, more than 2 million Americans had this disorder. This problem affects so many Americans that it's been called an epidemic, or an outbreak of a health problem that affects many people at one time.

People have different ideas about how to handle this problem and save as many lives as possible. Some believe people who illegally sell drugs should face stronger **punishments**. Others believe better health care is needed for people struggling with addiction to these deadly drugs.

## Facing the Facts

A medicine has been created that can save the lives of people who have overdosed on opioids. This is part of a way to fight drug abuse that's known as harm reduction, which works to stop people who abuse drugs from harming themselves and others.

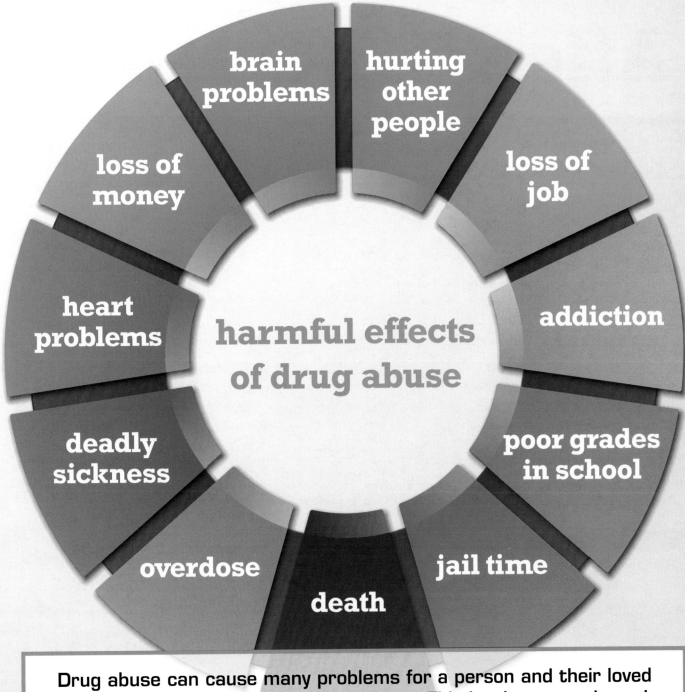

brain problems

hurting other people

loss of money

loss of job

harmful effects of drug abuse

heart problems

addiction

deadly sickness

poor grades in school

overdose

death

jail time

Drug abuse can cause many problems for a person and their loved ones, such as the problems shown here. This is why so much work is being done to help people with opioid use disorders and other substance use disorders.

# Affecting Others

Americans have started talking about drug abuse and addiction more openly because of the opioid epidemic. Many people hope this will lead to more people getting help for substance use disorders.

If a person is abusing drugs, it also affects their loved ones. It's good for family members and friends of people who abuse drugs to talk to someone about what they're going through. They can learn healthy ways to deal with the problems caused by a loved one's drug abuse and how to help their loved one get better.

## Facing the Facts 🔍

As of 2017, 46 percent of adults in the United States said they have a close friend or family member who's been addicted to drugs.

When a family member or friend is abusing drugs, people often blame themselves. Talking to a professional can help them understand that it's not their fault. It can also help them deal with anger, sadness, or fear, which are common things to feel when a loved one is abusing drugs.

# You Can Help!

Drug abuse and addiction are big problems, and hearing about them can make people feel afraid and hopeless—especially if someone they love is abusing drugs. However, with the right help and hard work, recovery is possible. This happens when a person stops using drugs and begins to live a healthier life.

Even the smallest actions can help in the fight against drug abuse. What can you do? You can start by choosing not to abuse drugs. You can also help others around you make that same choice.

## Facing the Facts

The Drug Abuse Resistance Education (D.A.R.E.) **program** was started in 1983 to help students learn about the dangers of drugs and how to be safe and responsible as they grow up. More than 1.5 million students go through D.A.R.E. programs every year.

D.A.R.E. TO RESIST DRUGS AND VIOLENCE.

# WHAT CAN YOU DO?

Choose not to abuse drugs.

Help others around you choose not to abuse drugs.

Follow your doctor's directions when you're given medicine.

If you're abusing drugs, ask for help.

If you think someone you know is abusing drugs, tell a trusted adult.

Raise money for groups that help people recover from addiction.

Listen to trusted adults and talk honestly with them about drug abuse.

If a loved one is abusing drugs, remember that it's not your fault.

Addiction is a scary sickness, and drug abuse is a big problem. However, you don't have to feel hopeless or helpless when faced with these issues. These are just a few of the things you can do to stay healthy and safe and help others do the same.

# GLOSSARY

**affect:** To produce an effect on something.

**chemical:** Matter that can be mixed with other matter to cause changes.

**cigarette:** A small roll of cut leaves wrapped in paper for smoking.

**electronic:** Working through the use of many small electrical parts.

**marijuana:** The dried leaves of the hemp plant that can be smoked to cause changes in the mind and body.

**professional:** A person who does a job that requires special education or skill.

**program:** A plan of action.

**protect:** To keep safe.

**punishment:** The act of making someone suffer for doing something wrong.

**responsibly:** Done in a safe way.

# FOR MORE INFORMATION

## WEBSITES

**Easy-to-Read Drug Facts**

*easyread.drugabuse.gov*

This website features videos and facts about drug abuse and the effects different drugs have on the body.

**"What You Need to Know About Drugs"**

*kidshealth.org/en/kids/know-drugs.html*

This KidsHealth article explains basic facts about drug abuse and addiction, and it also has links to other helpful articles.

## BOOKS

Etingoff, Kim. *Drugs and Alcohol.* Broomall, PA: Mason Crest, 2015.

Paris, Stephanie. *Drugs and Alcohol.* Huntington Beach, CA: Teacher Created Materials, 2012.

Raatma, Lucia. *Making Smart Choices.* Danbury, CT: Children's Press, 2013.

# INDEX